CHILDREN'S REFERENCE
MODERN HISTORY

Capella

This edition published in 2008 by Arcturus Publishing Limited
26/27 Bickels Yard, 151–153 Bermondsey Street,
London SE1 3HA

ISBN: 978-1-84193-824-0

Designers: Q2A India and Talking Design
Editors: Rebecca Gerlings and Alex Woolf

Printed in China

Contents

Introduction

In the sixteenth century, the world stood on the threshold of great changes that would carry it into the modern era. Europeans were discovering new lands and establishing powerful trading empires. Centuries-old ideas about the universe and our place in it were being challenged by a scientific revolution, and a new flowering in the arts was under way in the Renaissance. These changes, in turn, would lead to further upheaval in the centuries ahead. Scientific advances produced new technologies that would give rise to an industrial revolution in the 18th and 19th centuries, and a computer revolution in the 20th. Ideas about human rights, freedom, and equality would inspire political revolutions in France, America, and Russia. And rivalries between the great powers would eventually lead to two devastating world wars.

In this book, you will discover many fascinating facts about modern history. For example, do you know what European country established an empire that covered nearly one-third of the Earth's land surface? Who designed the world's first computer back in 1833? And which French emperor sold Louisiana to the USA for less than three cents an acre? You can find out the answers to these questions and many more in the pages of this book.

Colonial Empires

The 16th century was the beginning of an Age of Imperialism. European countries became rich and powerful because of their conquests and colonies in other continents. In fact, many places outside Europe were European colonies at some time.

British colonies   Spanish colonies
French colonies   Portugese colon...

▼ **A colonial ruler**
Queen Victoria represented the golden age of British colonialism.

▲ **Age of empire**
A map of the ma... powers during t... Colonial age.

Key facts:

• The English language is one of the major contributions the British Empire has made to the world. Today, it is the second most widely spoken language in the world, used in nearly 100 countries.

• In 1776, 13 British colonies in North America signed the Declaration of Independence. These colonies joined together to form the United States of America. They were the first British colonies to become independent.

• The European colonies of Canada, Australia, New Zealand, and the Union of South Africa were made dominions of the British Empire in the late 19th to early 20th centuries. This gave them the power to be completely independent.

• Today, the Falkland Islands, Gibraltar, and British Antarctic Territory are overseas territories of the United Kingdom.

• The French colonial empire was the world's second largest empire after the British. During the mid-19th century France established control over parts of Asia and North, West, and Central Africa.

When Europeans began discovering the countries in the East, the Caribbean, and the Americas, they found that these were sources of gold, spices, silk, sugar, slaves, and all kind of things that could make them rich. Portugal was the first country to establish colonies, in its neighboring Mediterranean islands of the Azores and Madeira, around the mid-1400s. Spain, Britain, France, Germany, and the Netherlands soon followed by colonizing parts of Africa, the Americas, India, and Southeast Asia. Early colonies, especially in Africa, were first established as trading posts that facilitated trade in slaves, and gold, ivory, and other exotic goods. Over the years, the European populations at these trading posts steadily increased and through a combination of war and peaceful treaties, the colonizers gained greater control of the colonies. Often the native populations turned to the European traders for support and protection from invading neighbors. Therefore, placed in a position of power, the European settlers took control of the administration and governance of these countries and declared them colonial territories of their respective countries. The colonial rulers collected taxes and controlled law and order, the court system, agriculture, industry, and trade in the colony.

British Empire

Britain was the largest imperial power between the 16th and 19th centuries. The British Empire extended over a large part of North America, large parts of Africa and the Middle East, India, Sri Lanka, some Southeast Asian countries, several South Pacific Islands, and all of Australia and New Zealand. That is nearly one-third of all the land in the world.

...pes of colonies

...ain dealt differently with each of her ...onies. In Asia and Africa, companies first ...blished trading posts, and after gaining ...trust of the native kings, began governing ...country. Eventually, the British monarch ...ld declare the region an imperial territory ...Britain. In some Middle Eastern countries ...ain was only a protector and the country ...its protectorate. This meant that the ...ntry had its own government, but was loyal ...he British crown and had to obey Britain ...ome matters. A third type of British colony ...populated only by settlers from England, ...later the United Kingdom. The first ...ong these was Newfoundland, followed by ...onies in the eastern parts of North ...erica, the Caribbean, and, later, Australia ...New Zealand.

...d of the Empire

...he 20th century, the Imperial Age ...lly came to an end with Britain's colonies ...anding independence. Britain, weakened ...he two World Wars, had to eventually give ...o the demands of the native populations ...ts colonies and grant them freedom. ...st of the other Asian and African countries ...gained independence by the 1960s.

Commonwealth

The Queen of England continues to be the queen of 16 former colonies, although she only holds the title and has no real powers. These 16 countries are called Commonwealth Realms. All countries that were once British colonies, including the Commonwealth Realms, are now part of the Commonwealth of Nations. There are 53 countries in this association, which co-operate and help each other in trade and development.

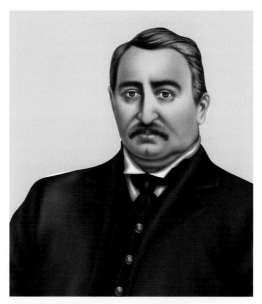

◀ **The great statesman**
Cecil Rhodes played a very important role in the British colonization of Africa. He helped Britain annex many of the South African states. He also proposed the famous "red line"—a railway network connecting all the British colonies from the north to the south of Africa. This railway line was supposed to help in the administration of the colonies as well as enable quick movement of troops through British territories. Rhodes also served as the Prime Minister of Cape Colony and founded the state of Rhodesia (modern Zambia and Zimbabwe).

◀ **Freedom at last**
India was the first British colony to become independent. It won its freedom on August 15, 1947, after about 40 years of struggle. Although India was led by many brave leaders throughout her struggle, Mahatma Gandhi was the most prominent of them all. It was his non-violent movement that finally drove the British out.

Try these too:

The Industrial Revolution (p 10–11),
Moving Ahead (p 12–13),
The American Revolution and Civil War (p 16–17)

The Industrial Revolution

During the 18th century, Western Europe underwent great change. The main way of earning a living shifted from farming to manufacturing, and from working with one's hands to working with machines. The Industrial Revolution began in Britain and spread to the rest of Europe and to North America.

▲ **Sowing the right way**
Jethro Tull's seed drill marked the beginning of mechanization in farming. Before that, farmers sowed by hand.

Key facts:

- One factor partly responsible for the Industrial Revolution was the excellent transportation system in Britain. Turnpike roads, navigable rivers, and canals, on which horse-drawn barges could sail, provided a good inland network, and ships sailed along the coast. These multiple transportation systems helped in swiftly transporting raw materials to factories and finished goods to cities and ports.

- The postage stamp was a significant Industrial Age invention. It led to the birth of the modern postal system. The first postage stamp was the Penny Black. It was introduced in 1840. The idea of introducing prepaid postage stamps at a very nominal cost of one penny was pioneered by Rowland Hill, a British teacher, in 1837.

- During the early part of the Industrial Revolution, Britain's gross domestic product or GDP (value of goods produced) was only £217 million (for the decade of 1800 to 1809). By 1869, British industries had raised the GDP to £633 million—an almost threefold increase within just 60 years.

Britain had good supplies of coal and iron, two of the most important materials used during the Industrial Revolution. The scientific discoveries and inventions of the 17th century paved the way for industrialization.

How it started
The earliest signs of industrialization were seen in agriculture. The invention of the seed drill, new crop rotation methods, and proper breeding of animals improved farming and made it more efficient.

Changing world
Until the mid-18th century, almost everything was handmade. However, handmade products could only be made in small numbers. As the population grew, it became necessary to find ways to manufacture large quantities quickly. Machines were invented to do this.

Iron, coal, and steam
An important step in the development of machines was the discovery of ways to use c and iron. Iron could be made into hard an strong sheets, which could be used to make machines. Coal was used to produce heat a steam energy, which was used to power the machines. Steam was the most important source of energy in 18th-century England.

An early steam engine was made by Thor Savery, an English engineer, in 1689, to pum water out of coal mines. Later, Scottish engine James Watt designed a steam engine that co be used to run various kinds of machines.

▶ **Finding work**
The workers moved to cities to find jobs in the factories that had sprung up.

xtile industry

e textile industry in England changed
1ost completely because of the Industrial
 olution. Until then, wool, linen, and flax
 were spun by hand and the yarn was
 n used to weave cloth on handlooms. All
 changed in the 18th century, with the
 ;inning of industrialization. In 1733, John
  invented the flying shuttle, which partly
 chanized the weaving process. Then in
 '0, British industrialist James Hargreaves
 ented the spinning jenny. This machine
 ıld spin several threads at the same time.
 e third invention that changed the textile
 ustry was the water-powered spinning
 ne designed by Richard Arkwright.
 ould produce even stronger thread for
 1. However, it was only with the invention
 he "mule" by Samuel Crompton, in 1779,
 t good-quality yarn was made. Now English
 tiles could be made more cheaply and
 ckly than anywhere else in the world.

"Watt" an invention!

es Watt's steam engine was largely reponsible for
 advent of the Industrial Revolution.

Better quality and higher production of
garments did not mean better working
conditions for laborers. There was no
proper health care or safety
regulations for workers. Factory
owners employed a large
number of children as
they worked hard
and for less money.
This situation did
not change until
the end of the
19th century.

▸ Revolutionary invention

The spinning jenny
revolutionized the textile
industry. This device could
spin several threads at the
same time, reducing the
amount of time and work
required to produce yarn.
With the invention of the
jenny, a worker could
now make eight or
more spools at once.

Try these too:

Moving Ahead (p 12–13),
The Scientific
Revolution (p 14–15),
The Computer
Revolution (p 24–25)

Wedgwood

**English pottery was yet another industry that benefited
from the Industrial Revolution. Potter and designer Josiah
Wedgwood set up a partly mechanized factory in Staffordshire,
which produced a range of ware. The machines that mixed
and ground raw materials ran on power generated by
waterwheels and windmills. By 1850, the manufacture
of pottery was extensively mechanized.**

Moving Ahead

By about 1850, the second stage of the Industrial Revolution had begun. The most important developments of this time were the steam powered locomotive and the railways. Steam engines were also used on ships. Among the key inventions were the internal combustion engine and electricity.

▼ Setting the standard
In 1829, George Stephenson and his son, Robert, built the first modern steam locomotive, the *Rocket*. The new locomotive had many revolutionary features that were adapted into all steam locomotives built after it. A replica of the *Rocket* can be seen at the Science Museum in London.

The very first railway was a horse-drawn cart pulled along wooden rails. By the late 1700s, iron rails began to be widely used by most coal mines to transport coal. The English engineer Richard Trevithick invented the first steam locomotive, which was not very successful. In 1814, George Stephenson designed a successful steam locomotive, *Active* (which was later renamed *Locomotion*). This engine ran on rails and became the first steam locomotive ever to be used for public travel in 1825, when the Stockton and Darlington Railway employed its services. The company opened the railway to people who wanted to travel on its 26-mile (40-kilometer) route. The first successful steamship was designed by Robert Fulton, an American engineer. In 1807, Fulton inaugurated his boat, the *North River Steamboat*, with a trip down the Hudson River, from New York to Albany. Soon after, the steamboat began a regular passenger service.

▶ Picture perfect
The first practical process of photography was made public in 1839, by Frenchman Louis Daguerre. A picture was recorded on a metal plate coated with silver iodide. The plate was treated with mercury fumes and preserved by applying salt.

By the time the second phase was in full swing, Britain had lost its monopoly to the United States and Germany. The main trigg[er] for the second phase was developments in the fields of electricity, communication, and transport. In the United States, the pioneer[s] included such great names as Thomas Alva Edison, George Westinghouse, and Nikola Tesla. If steam engines dominated the first phase, it was the internal combustion engin[e] that drove the second one. German invento[rs] Gottlieb Daimler and Nikolaus August Otto were the forces behind this new wave, while American businessman Henry Ford's assembly line revolutionized factory production like never before.

und and light

831, Michael Faraday, the famous British
ntist, devised a method to generate
ctricity, and by 1881 American inventor
omas Alva Edison was able to mass produce
andescent light bulbs. Meanwhile, Nikola
la invented electric transformers that
ld produce alternating current. However,
as only in 1891 that the first long-distance,
h-powered transmission system was made.
rge Westinghouse built it for use in a
d mine in Colorado.

In 1876, Alexander Graham Bell changed
way the world communicated by inventing
telephone. It was the first time, speech was
verted to sound waves and sent through a
e to a receiver. By 1877, sound could also
recorded. Edison's phonograph could not
y record sound, but also play it back.

Steel

Civilizations have grown and flourished
because of the way in which they used metal.
Starting from the Iron Age, metal has been
important to man for its use in making
farming tools, weapons, building
equipment, and for use in ornaments and
currency. The invention of steel in the 1850s
and 1860s was an important development.
Steel was to become the metal of the modern
world. Henry Bessemer and William Siemens
were responsible for designing methods and
equipment through which good quality steel
could be produced in large quantities.

▶ **"Watson, I need you!"**
Alexander Graham Bell's
first telephonic conversation
was believed to have been
with his assistant, Watson.

▼ **Car for the masses**
The Ford Model T was the first truly
affordable car. It was also the first car
to be mass produced on assembly lines.

RT 2356

Key facts:

• Thomas Alva Edison
was probably one of
the busiest inventors
of the second
Industrial Revolution.
He had 1,093 design
patents in his name.
However, not all of his
designs were original.
Many of them were
improvements on
designs by others.

• In the late-19th
century, railways were
combined with
electricity to make
electric "streetcars."
By the end of the
century, electricity was
available everywhere
and streetcars became
popular in many big
cities of the world.

Try these too:

The Industrial Revolution
(p 10–11), The Scientific
Revolution (p 14–15),
The Computer
Revolution (p 24–25)

Macadam roads

Modern roads were invented by a renowned
Scottish engineer named John Loudon
McAdam. This enterprising inventor
realized that it was important for roads to
be higher than their surrounding area and
that they should have smooth and hard
surfaces to make them safe and easy to
travel on. Therefore, McAdam made roads
using a mixture of gravel and rock, with side
ditches for drainage. The entire surface was
compacted and fine gravel was added to bind
it. This method is called macadamization.

The Scientific Revolution

Man has always been curious about the world around him. Knowledge about the natural world has helped scientists discover and invent things that have changed and improved our lives. Although the study of science can probably be dated to the time early man started observing the various phenomena of nature, it was in the 16th and 17th centuries that some of the greatest scientific discoveries took place.

Key facts:

• The words "science" and "scientist" were not in use when the Scientific Revolution began. People studying science were called natural philosophers.

• The study of the motion of bodies under the influence of forces, pioneered by Galileo, Brahe, Kepler, and Newton, is called classical mechanics.

• Galileo Galilei was an inventor as well as an astronomer. He invented a surveyor's compass and the thermometer, and vastly improved the telescope and the microscope. He also made designs for an automatic tomato picker, and a device with a candle and mirror, which could reflect light through an entire building.

▶ **Kepler's discovery**
In 1604, Johannes Kepler observed a luminous stellar explosion in the sky. This proved that nothing in the Universe was indestructible. On the contrary, the Universe was constantly changing. The bright explosion of the star, called "Kepler's supernova," was the last supernova observed in the Milky Way.

In the earliest civilizations of Mesopotamia, Egypt, China, and the Indus Valley, people studied the movement of the Sun and Moon. They also laid the foundations of early mathematics and medicine. In Ancient Greece, philosophers Aristotle and Plato showed a deep interest in physics, while Ptolemy made his mark in astronomy and the movement of planets. Pythagoras studied mathematics and geometry and Hippocrates conducted research in medicine. Their work and study, and that of several other unknown scientists, formed the basis upon which modern science has developed.

Astronomy

Polish astronomer and mathematician Nicolaus Copernicus was the first to discover that the Sun was at the center of the solar system and not the Earth, as people had believed all along. His work was further developed by scientists like Tycho Brahe and Johannes Kepler, who confirmed the theory.

Kepler explained how planets move on elliptical paths. Italian astronomer Galileo Galilei observed sunspots on the Sun and craters and mountains on the Moon. He also discovered that Jupiter had several moons that revolved around it. These first moons, observed by him, were named the Galilean moons in his honor.

Physics

As well as astronomy, Galileo also had an interest in physics. He conducted experiments to study the movement of objects and devised a method to measure their speed. He also conducted experiments to measure the speed of light. However, it was Ole Rømer, the Danish astronomer, who first proved that the speed of light is finite. The study of motion was continued by English physicist Sir Isaac Newton. This great scientist also studied light and explained gravitational force.

▼ **A scientist par excellence**
Galileo is regarded as the father of astronomy and modern physics for his contributions in these fields.

...thematics

...e French philosopher and mathematician ...é Descartes was the first person to ...nonstrate that algebra and geometry ...e not two completely separate branches ...mathematics, but actually inseparably ...nected. He showed how problems in ...ebra could be converted and solved using ...metry, and vice versa. Isaac Newton's ...portant contributions are the binomial ...orem and calculus, both important ...ects of modern mathematics.

...logy

...glish scientist Robert Hooke invented a ...hly precise compound microscope with ...ch he was able to study plants and animals. ...coined the word *cell*, while studying the ...ucture of plants because he thought that ...nt cells looked very much like monks' ...s in a monastery. In 1796, Edward Jenner ...de an important contribution to medical ...nce when he invented the first vaccine. ...e vaccine was responsible for putting an ...d to smallpox, which was a widespread ...d dreaded disease at that time.

...emistry

...eral elements like magnesium, nickel, ...ogen, chlorine, tungsten, zirconium, and ...nium were discovered during the 18th ...tury. French chemist Antoine Lavoisier ...onsidered to be the father of modern ...mistry. In the 1770s, he proved that ...gen, the gas responsible for life, was also ...ponsible for burning and rusting. He also ...wed that oxygen combined with hydrogen ...duced water. Later, he published the first ...dern chemistry textbook with a list of ...stances and elements.

▲ **The Newton effect**
According to popular legend, Newton was sitting under an apple tree, when an apple fell down. He wondered why the apple had fallen down and not gone up or sideways. He soon discovered that gravity was the answer.

▲ **The medical eye**
The compound microscope is an indispensable instrument in modern medicine.

▲ **Better than cure**
Jenner injected a boy with cowpox, which was not a fatal disease. He then innoculated the boy with smallpox. The boy did not fall sick and became the first to be vaccinated.

...aconian method

...ir Francis Bacon, the Lord Chancellor of ...ngland during the rule of James I, was a ...cholar and writer. In 1606, he published ...book called *Novum Organum*, which ...xplained the manner in which scientific experiments and research should be carried out. He believed that to gain a complete and correct understanding of science, it was necessary to experiment repeatedly and to carefully make observations.

Try these too:

The Industrial Revolution (p 10–11), Moving Ahead (p 12–13), The Computer Revolution (p 24–25), The Modern World (p 26–27)

The American Revolution and Civil Wa

The American War of Independence (or the American Revolution) and the Civil War were the most important events in the early history of the United States. The Revolution led to freedom from Britain and the formation of the country, and the Civil War marked the end of slavery in the United States.

Key facts:

• The United States Constitution was adopted in March 1789. However, the situation was not very stable and for years many states resented the federal government's control over them. The election of Abraham Lincoln as President, in 1861, led to the culmination of this bitterness in the American Civil War.

• The world's first submarine was used by the Continental Navy on September 6, 1776, to sink a British ship. The attempt failed, however. The submarine, called *Turtle*, was designed by David Bushnell, an American inventor. It was made up of two shell-like parts of oak, coated with tar.

• While the Confederacy and Union were fighting the Civil War, President Lincoln issued the Emancipation Proclamation on January 1, 1863. The proclamation stated that all slaves in the Confederate States were free. A million copies of this proclamation were distributed among the slaves in the south to spread the word and start trouble in Confederacy camps.

Until about the mid-1700s most American colonists were content to be subjects of Britain. However, from 1764 onward, Britain passed a series of acts that the American colonists found intolerable. With these acts the British government increased taxes and import duties on a wide range of commodities including sugar, indigo dye, wine, textiles, paper, and tea. They also imposed taxes on all printed material such as documents, pamphlets, newspapers, and even playing cards.
Britain also did not allow the United States to print their own currency notes. Angered by Britain's high handedness, the colonists decided to revolt against Britain.

Events of the revolution

The colonists formed the Continental Army, to take on the British might. They also hastily put a navy together. To begin with, the Continental Army and navy lost every battle as they did not have enough people, money, or arms. However, France came to the aid of the Americans by sending them money, ammunition, and even troops.

▶ **Charismatic leader**
George Washington's contribution in the Revolution has led to him being regarded as the father of the nation.

Britain was supported by several native tribes who hated the white colonists. A num of battles were fought and a lot of lives wer lost on both sides before the British force surrendered on October 19, 1781. In April 1782, the British Parliament voted to end th war in America and on September 3, 1783, Britain and America signed the Treaty of P to officially end the American Revolution.

▼ **Party at sea**
The Boston Tea Party took place on the night of December 16, 1773, as an act of protest against the Act. About 60 revolutionaries went aboard three Bri ships anchored at the Boston Harbor, and dumped t cargo of 342 boxes of tea into the sea.

il war

en Abraham Lincoln was elected President
he United States in 1861, he announced
intention to end slavery in the country.
southern states were not happy to hear
. The plantations in these states depended
vily on slave labor. They decided that the
y way to take care of their interests was to
e the Union. South Carolina was the first
e to secede from the Union. Florida,
sissippi, Georgia, Texas, Alabama,
iisiana, Tennessee, North Carolina,
ginia, and Arkansas soon joined them.
se 11 seceded states formed the
nfederate States of America and elected
erson Davis as their President. This
alled the start of the Civil War. The war
fought between 23 federal states, most of
ch formed the northern part of the
ited States, and the 11 confederate
thern states. The Confederacy raised an
iy and began the war in April 1861. They
cked Fort Sumter in North Carolina and
cessfully took control of it. President
coln responded by cutting off all supplies
he southern states. In 1863, Lincoln
ased the Emancipation Proclamation that
all slaves, including the ones in the
thern states, free. The war was waged with
eral successes and failures on both sides.
wever, the Federal army, which was more
verful and better equipped, was eventually
e to outlast its opponents. After four years
ierce fighting, the Confederates ran out of
plies and troops. Finally, on April 9, 1865,
Confederate troops gave up the fight and
rendered. The seceded states eventually
ined the United States of America.

◀ The great general
Ulysses S. Grant is most remembered for his contribution and strategies during the American Civil War. He was solely responsible for the Union victory at Vicksburg, Mississippi, which eventually turned the tables on the Confederate States. General Grant also forced the surrender of Robert E. Lee, the most successful Confederate general, at Appomattox, Virginia, effectively ending the Civil War. Later, in 1869, Grant became the president of the United States. However, he is considered to be one of the worst presidents as his administration was filled with corrupt officials.

▲ The death of a president
On April 14, 1865, after the Confederates had surrendered, President Abraham Lincoln and the First Lady celebrated by going to see a play. During the play, the president was shot dead by a Confederate supporter named John Wilkes Booth.

Declaration of Independence

The *American Declaration of Independence* was drafted by a committee specially appointed for the purpose by Congress. Thomas Jefferson, Benjamin Franklin, John Adams, Roger Sherman, and Robert Livingston were the members of this committee. Jefferson wrote ut the first draft of the declaration, and Adams and Franklin made some changes to it. On June 28, 1776, Jefferson's *Declaration of Independence* was presented to Congress, which hen formally endorsed the Declaration on July 4, 1776, and sent copies to all the 3 colonies. The colonies signed the declaration, announcing their freedom, but Britain efused to accept her defeat until October 19, 1781.

Try these too:

Colonial Empires (p 8–9),
The Industrial Revolution (p 10–11),
Moving Ahead (p12–13),
The French Revolution (p 18–19),
The First World War and the Russian Revolution (p 20–21)

The French Revolution

The French Revolution was one of the most important events in the history of Europe. It took place between 1789 and 1799 and completely changed the face of French society and politics.

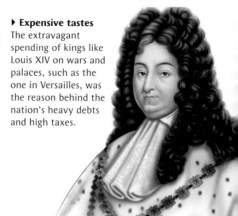

▶ **Expensive tastes**
The extravagant spending of kings like Louis XIV on wars and palaces, such as the one in Versailles, was the reason behind the nation's heavy debts and high taxes.

Key facts:

- In 1803, Napoleon realized that it was impossible for him to defend French territories in America while he was busy fighting wars at home. In a deal called the Louisiana Purchase, Napoleon sold the Louisiana territory to the United States, at less than three cents an acre ($7 per square kilometer).

- The Napoleonic Code is the set of civil laws formulated by Napoleon in 1804. It was the first successful system to codify European civil law and is still followed in many countries.

- A major factor that influenced the French citizens to begin a revolution was the 18th century movement called the Enlightenment. During this period, philosophers like Voltaire and Rousseau encouraged progress and scientific thought and looked down upon the old traditions and superstitions that were promoted by the Church and the state.

By the 18th century, the population of France had grown to 25 million people, the largest in Europe at that time. Most of these people were poor peasants who lived in villages. Paris was crowded, filled with merchants, traders, and factory workers who felt that the king and the nobility had all the privileges while the people had nothing. Taxes were high, food was scarce and the country was deep in debt. Unhappy with their situation and unwilling to tolerate it, the people of France rose up in a revolt against the monarchy.

Angry mobs

On July 14, 1789, an angry mob stormed the Bastille prison in Paris and set some of its prisoners free in a show of rebellion against their king. This spirit of revolt soon spread through the country. A National Assembly was formed as the common man's government. It did away with the feudalistic landowning system and reduced the privileges of the nobility. On August 26, 1789, the Assembly published the *Declaration of the Rights of Man and of the Citizen,* which gave equal rights and freedom to all Frenchmen.

The Republic

In August 1792, Louis XVI was forced to step down from the throne. His family was imprisoned and France was declared a republic. The following year he was tried and executed by the guillotine. It was a time of widespread rioting in the country and food was still scarce. France was also at war with many of its neighboring countries. Various factions began revolting against the National Convention, the governing body of the new Republic. The National Convention, in turn, tried to subdue the opposition. Finally, the Convention was disbanded in October 1795. In the same year, the Republic was ended as the Directory, headed by five directors, took control. The Directory was replaced by the Consulate in 1799, when Napoleon Bonaparte, the French army general, overthrew it and proclaimed himself the first consul of France.

▶ **Storming of the Bastille**
The revolutionaries seized the prison and killed its commander, Bernard de Launay, and many of his guards. The event was significant as it was the first open rebellion against the king.

Guillotine

The guillotine was a device used for executing prisoners who were given the death sentence. It was first used on April 25, 1792, to execute a French highwayman and was the only legal method of execution in France until the death penalty was abolished in 1981. At least 20,000 people are estimated to have been executed by the guillotine during the French Revolution. The guillotine was used to execute protestors during the Reign of Terror, from 1793 to 1794.

Napoleonic era

Napoleon was one of France's most successful military generals and led the French army successfully in many battles. As a dictator and as emperor after 1804, he brought most of Western and Central Europe under his control. He was also an excellent statesman. He made the government more centralized and efficient, improved education, taxation, banking, sanitation, and law and order.

The fall of Napoleon

It was Napoleon's ambition to conquer the whole of Europe that eventually caused his downfall. Napoleon's 1812 invasion of Russia ended in a humiliating defeat. His offensive on Germany met with an even worse fate, when he was forced to retreat in the Battle of Leipzig in 1813. The following year, Britain, Russia, Prussia, and Austria joined forces and captured Paris. Napoleon was arrested and exiled to the Mediterranean island of Elba. He escaped in less than 11 months and returned to Paris in March 1815, where he was restored to the throne. However, in June, he was defeated by the Duke of Wellington in the Battle of Waterloo. He was then exiled to the island of St Helena, where he died in 1821.

▼ **A stinging defeat**
In 1812, Napoleon led an army of almost 700,000 men into Russia. Lack of food, the bitter Russian winter, and other logistical problems forced the French army to eventually retreat. Only 22,000 men survived the campaign.

Try these too:

Colonial Empires (p 8–9), The American Revolution and Civil War (p 16–17), The First World War and the Russian Revolution (p 20–21)

North America

South America

Louisiana

▲ **Louisiana purchased!**
In 1803, Napoleon sold the French Louisiana territory to the United States for 15 million dollars. It included the present state of Louisiana, all or parts of Missouri, Iowa, North and South Dakota, Texas, Kansas, and Colorado.

The First World War and the Russian Revolution

The First World War was fought between 1914 and 1918. It was the biggest and most violent war Europe had ever experienced. The First World War involved the United States as well as most of the countries in the European continent. It was also a period of great political upheaval and change. The monarchies of Germany and Austria-Hungary, and the kingdom of the Ottomans, collapsed as a result of this war.

▼ Trench warfare
The heavy loss of life in the Western Front trenches is one of the most unforgettable horrors of the First World War. Thousands of soldiers were killed by firearms and poison gas, while many more died after contracting infections.

In Russia especially, the war had a profound effect. The old order ended and a Communist government came to power in 1917, following a series of political and social uprisings called the Russian Revolution.

The players

The First World War was also known as the Great War. It was fought between the Allied Powers and the Central Powers. The major Allied countries were Britain (and its colonies), Russia, Japan, and the United States. The Central Powers included Germany, Austria-Hungary, Bulgaria, and the Ottoman Empire. By the 20th century, European politics had become extremely complicated, with monarchs and leaders having treaties, agreements, and secret understandings with some countries and long-standing disputes with others. This had fostered a great deal of suspicion and mistrust among various nations.

The war begins

The event that triggered the war was the assassination of Franz Ferdinand, heir to the Austria-Hungary throne, by a Serbian student. This incident prompted Austria-Hungary to declare war on Serbia. Russia joined the war in support of Serbia, and Germany got involved in support of Austria France and Britain, being allies of Russia, a joined the war. In 1917, the United States joined the battle by declaring war against Germany. Finally, after four years of intense fighting, peace was declared on November 1918. The war resulted in the separation of Hungary from Austria, the formation of Czechoslovakia and Yugoslavia, and the independence of Poland after more than a century of foreign domination by Austria, Prussia, and Russia. Germany was forced to give up about 10 percent of its territories ar all of its overseas colonies, reduce the size c its military, and pay huge amounts in compensation to the Allies.

▼ Participants of the war
The map shows the European military alliances during the First World War. The green regions represent the Allied forces, or Entente Powers, while the orange portion represents the Central Powers, so called beca they were located between Russia, France, and Britai The countries marked in grey were neutral.

Zeppelins

Zeppelins were gigantic German airships that were used for bombing and scouting during the First World War. The first ever Zeppelin air raid on Britain took place on the night of January 19, 1915. Germany built 88 Zeppelins during the war and carried out more than 50 successful air raids on Britain.

▼ **Communist Russia**
As the leader of the Bolshevik Party, Vladimir Ilyich Lenin became the first Premier of the Soviet Union when the party came to power following the October Revolution.

The Russian Bolshevik Revolution

The Russian Revolution refers to three separate events. The first revolution took place in 1905. It was marked by a series of riots protesting against the rule of Tsar Nicholas II. This revolution was not very successful, but is seen as a trigger for the revolution of 1917. The 1917 revolution was a historical movement that can be divided into two parts—the February Revolution in 1917 and the October Revolution in the same year. The Russian people had grown increasingly unhappy with the dictatorial rule of Tsar Nicholas II, the feudalistic system in the country, and the scarcity of food and extreme poverty that had resulted from the fighting in the First World War. In February 1917, the people of Petrograd, the capital city, began protesting against the tsar. They were joined by soldiers who went on strike and refused to continue in the war. The tsar was finally forced to give up his throne and a temporary government was formed. However, this government was weak and ineffective and, in October, the Communist Bolshevik group, led by Vladimir Lenin, took control of the Russian government. The Communists believed that all citizens had equal rights and responsibilities and that everyone should work for the benefit of the state. This model lasted for about 70 years. It was also copied in other countries, including China and Cuba.

Try these too:

Colonial Empires (p 8–9),
The Second World War (p 22–23),
The Modern World (p 26–27)

▶ **The end of a dynasty**
Nicholas II was forced to abdicate on March 2, 1917, bringing 300 years of Romanov rule to an end. The Tsar and his family were kept under house arrest until July 17, 1918, when they were executed by a group of Bolshevik secret police led by Yakov Yurovsky.

Key facts:

• Nearly nine million soldiers died on the battlefield during the First World War. Almost the same number, or more, civilians died in various countries during that time due to food shortages, being caught up in battle, air raids, or mass killing by enemy troops.

• The First World War witnessed the first appearance of many modern combat techniques, including trenches, aircraft, poison gas, tanks, and machine guns.

• The event that triggered the Russian Revolution of 1905 was the Bloody Sunday massacre on January 22, 1905. A group of factory workers gathered in front of the Winter Palace in St Petersburg to present a petition to the tsar. The Imperial Guards opened fire on the unarmed protesters, killing more than 100 people and injuring several more.

The Second World War

The Second World War was the largest and deadliest war in the history of the world. It was fought between 1939 and 1945 and involved almost all the nations that fought in the First World War. It was fought in Europe, Africa, Asia, and the Pacific.

Key facts:

- A new and highly effective military tactic introduced by the Germans in the Second World War was the blitzkrieg. A blitzkrieg involved making a swift and intense surprise attack on enemy camps or cities.

- At least 50 million people lost their lives in the Second World War. About six million of these were killed in the Holocaust, most of whom were Jews. Several million people became homeless and nearly 70 percent of Europe's industries were destroyed.

- When the war ended, the US Secretary of State, George Marshall drew up the Marshall Plan, according to which the US Congress contributed several billion dollars to help in the reconstruction of Europe.

- The Japanese feared that the presence of the US Navy in the Pacific would interfere with their military expansion. In an attempt to discourage US involvement in the war, Japan launched a suprise attack on the US naval base at Pearl Harbor, Hawaii. Japanese aircraft bombed the base on December 7, 1941, killing about 3,000 American soldiers.

The outbreak of the Second World War is attributed to the territorial ambitions of the German dictator, Adolf Hitler, who was responsible for widespread genocide and other atrocities both before and during the war.

Why war broke out

Germany and Japan were rising powers, ambitious to increase their power and territories. Imperial Japan, led by its military generals, took over Manchuria, Korea, and many parts of China. Germany, headed by Adolf Hitler, began expanding its control over neighboring territories. Italy was ruled by the fascist leader Benito Mussolini, who entered into an agreement with Germany to co-operate in all military matters. Later, Japan also signed co-operation treaties with both of these countries. Japan feared the growing power of the United States in the Pacific islands and launched an attack that eventually drew the latter into the war. In short, the atmosphere at that time was one of suspicion, fear, and hatred, which ultimately led to war.

The Allies

The opponents in the war were the Axis and Allied Powers. The Axis nations of Germany, fascist Italy, and Japan were later joined by Bulgaria, Romania, Hungary, Croatia, and Slovakia. The three main Allies were Britain, Russia, and the United States. They were supported by France, other European countries, the Commonwealth nations, China, and a few South American countries.

▶ **The stage is set**
The top map shows the political division of territories between the Allied (Britain, Russia, France, and United States) and the Axis Powers (Germany, Italy, Japan, and their allies) during the war. The bottom map depicts the drastic change that came about in the world map, following the defeat of the Axis Powers.

The mighty war

The war began on September 3, 1939, after Germany invaded Poland on September 1. There were two main theaters to the war—Western and Pacific. In the Pacific, the war was mainly fought between the United states and Japan, while on the Western front the Allied forces battled the combined might of Germany, Italy, and their allies. The death and destruction caused by this war surpassed anything that had ever taken place before. Horrifying new techniques like biological warfare, concentration camps, and atomic bombs, as well as advanced weapons and equipment such as rockets, jet aircraft, radar, and torpedoes were used. Eventually, Germany surrendered and the war in Europe officially ended on May 8, 1945. In Asia, fighting continued until Japan officially surrendered on September 2, 1945.

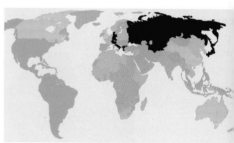

January 1, 1941

- ▢ Allied nations
- ▢ Allied occupied territory
- ■ Axis
- ▢ Axis occupied territory

January 1, 1945

◀ **The lethal mushroom**
The large greyish-purple mushroom cloud that loomed over Nagasaki after the atomic bombing rose about 11 miles (18 kilometers) from the point of impact. The cloud has now become a symbol of nuclear fallout.

Try these too:

Moving Ahead (p 12–13),
The Scientific
Revolution (p 14–15),
The First World War and
the Russian Revolution
(p 22–23),
The Modern World
(p 26–27)

he camps of no return
worst atrocities during the war were committed in
Nazi concentration camps, where millions of people
e, starved, tortured, and mass executed.

termath
e United States and the Soviet Union
erged as the two most powerful countries
er the Second World War. Most countries in
stern Europe formed democratic
vernments or continued with their pre-war
vernments. Countries in the east, which
re allies of the Soviet Union, naturally
came Communist countries. Germany
s divided into East and West Germany.
st Germany was brought under Soviet
e, and various parts of West Germany were
cupied by Britain, France, and America.
an lost all of its territories and powers and
s occupied by the Allies. Korea, which was
der Japanese rule until the end of the war,
s divided into two parts—North and South
rea. North Korea came under the control
the Communist Soviet Union, while its
uthern counterpart was occupied by the
ited States. This arrangement was politically
atile and eventually led to the Korean War.

wo of a kind
ler and Benito Mussolini, the fascist Italian leader,
red radical views. Therefore, it was only natural that
two countries struck an alliance during the war.
ch leaders were intolerant and merciless toward their
mies. They also resorted to violent methods to
ppress any uprising within their countries.

Hiroshima and Nagasaki

The first and the only time nuclear weapons were employed in a war was in 1945, when the United States bombed the Japanese cities of Hiroshima and Nagasaki. Hiroshima was bombed on August 6, while Nagasaki was bombed on August 9. At least 120,000 civilians died immediately after the attack. Since then, several thousands more have died due to radiation poisoning.

The Computer Revolution

The computer was the most revolutionary invention of the 20th century. The scientific developments of the 16th and 17th centuries, along with the industrial advances of the 18th century, created the need for an efficient and safe means of storing as well as processing information. Moreover, it became necessary to solve sophisticated formulae and compute complex calculations in a quicker and easier manner than already existed.

Key facts:

- There are three main categories of computers. The first includes mainframe computers, used by big companies and institutions to process a large amount of data. They are bulky and occupy entire rooms. The second includes minicomputers or workstations, accessed by multiple users. The third type is the personal computer or microcomputer used by an individual.

- A supercomputer is a particularly efficient and fast computer that is much more advanced than others of its type and time. The first one was designed by Seymour Cray in the 1960s. Today supercomputers are custom-made by large corporations.

- The computer is able to process information fed into it because of its software. A software consists of a specially encoded set of instructions called a programme. They control various parts of the computer. They also interact with human beings, process information and communicate with other software in the machine.

Computing devices like adding machines, calculators, and, later, the computer were developed to provide solutions to these problems. The first mechanical computer was invented by Wilhelm Schickard of Germany as early as 1623. It had wheels and cogs, like a clock, and could add and subtract six-digit numbers. However, it is Charles Babbage, an English professor, who is credited with designing the first modern computer in 1833. This machine, called the Analytical Engine, was supposed to add in 3 seconds and multiply and divide in 2–3 minutes, powered by steam. Unfortunately, it was never made as Babbage died before completing work on it.

Birth of the computer

By the early 1900s, people were using adding machines, cash registers, and mechanical computers, operated by electricity. These early computers had to be reset manually every time a new problem had to be

▲ Adding up
Calculators differ from computers in that they are used for specific operations, like mathematical calculations. Modern calculators run on batteries or solar energy and are pocket-sized

calculated. During the Second World War, there were rapid improvements in the desig of computing devices. The ENIAC, built for the US military during the war, was the first digital computer. It occupied about 1,800 square feet (168 square meters) of area and worked day and night solving problems. At this time, most computers were huge, almost as big as a small house. They could naturally only be used in government offices, by universities for research, and by large corporations.

Tough and reliable
Mainframe computers, referred to as Big Iron, extremely reliable, high secure, and durable. Th computers can continu to work uninterrupted several years. They can even be kept running while undergoing repai making them invaluabl large corporations whe any loss of time can seriously affect profits. Reliability, Availability, and Serviceability (or R. is the marketing term u to describe the qualities of mainframe computer

...mputer revolution

...e widespread use of computers began only ...er technological developments in the 1950s ...1 60s, which made them more accessible ...ordinary people. Computers became ...eractive—they played music and games ...d had magnetic memories that could ...re information. Computer languages ...e FORTRAN, COBOL, and BASIC were ...veloped. The floppy disk, printer, and ...use were invented, and computers were ...uipped for word processing.

...In 1975, the Intel Corporation designed ...air 8800, the first successful personal ...mputer. This was followed in 1977 by ...Apple II, designed by Steven Jobs and ...phen Wozniak. The Apple II was the ...t computer with a keyboard and a color ...play monitor. Jobs and Wozniak later ...nded the Apple Corporation. The highly ...cessful Apple Macintosh followed in 1984. ...1982, the first portable computer was ...roduced by Compaq, and in 1985 the ...t version of Microsoft Windows was ...nched. By this time, computers had ...come indispensable in commercial ...ablishments, institutions, and even homes. ...wever, it was with the invention of the ...rld Wide Web in 1989 that the computer ...ly revolutionized information processing, ...rage, and transfer. The computer had ...olved far beyond its original role as a ...culating and problem-solving machine. ...vas now capable of communication.

Contemporary devices

Computing devices took yet another huge leap forward with the invention of the cellular phone and handheld devices like the palm pilot and pocket PC. Cellular phones were originally only meant to be used as mobile telephones. However, today they are mobile computers that store and process information, allow access to the Internet, play music, and take and store photographs and video clips. Personal digital assistants (PDAs), or palm pilots, and pocket PCs offer many of the same features as mobile phones, but are not able to function as a telephone. Besides being versatile, these handheld devices can be used more conveniently as they can be carried easily and used almost anywhere.

▼ Surf on!

Internet cafes, also known as cyber cafes, offer Internet access for a fee. The concept and name was first proposed by Ivan Pope, a British computer professional. The first commercial Internet cafe was opened in London on September 1, 1994. A typical Internet cafe would consist of several computer stations connected to a common server, or LAN. Many people preferred Internet cafes as they were cheaper than owning a computer.

Try these too:

Moving Ahead (p 12–13), The Scientific Revolution (p 14–15), The Modern World (p 26–27), The New Millennium (p 28–29)

Bank any time
As in most fields, computers play an important role in banking. If it were not for computers, there would not be ATMs, which help use of banking facilities like withdrawing and depositing money any time or date we choose.

Computer games

The first computer game was developed in 1952 at the University of Cambridge, by A. S. Douglas. It was a game of tic tac toe, or noughts and crosses, and was called *OXO*. The first handheld game, made in 1972, was also *Tic Tac Toe*. It had nine buttons, which would flash red or green when pushed.

The Modern World

Following the devastating Second World War, many countries spent the latter part of the 20th century recovering from their losses, both economical and political, and reorganizing. Most colonies gained independence, and monarchies gave way to dictatorships, communism, or democracy.

▲ **A tale of grit**
Aung San Suu Kyi, the Burmese activist who has been fighting for democracy in her country, was placed under house arrest by the Myanmar military government in 1989. She was later released in 1995, only to be arrested again in 2003. Suu Kyi continues her struggle from within the confines of her house.

Key facts:

• The Soviet Union collapsed in 1991 as a result of the process of modernization begun by the Soviet President Mikhail Gorbachev. Ironically, this modernization broke the Soviet Union apart instead of improving it, as people demanded a complete change and break from communism.

• In 1945, the United Nations was formed with a membership of 51 countries. It is an international organization that helps to promote peace, safety, and development throughout the world.

• The Cold War between the United States and the Soviet Union was an important event that affected several countries around the world. The conflict, which began in 1947, divided the countries of the world into two groups—US supporters and Soviet supporters. It ended with the collapse of the Soviet Union in 1991.

▶ **The wall of separation**
The Berlin Wall, symbolic of the Cold War division of Europe, was a 96-mile (155-kilometer) long separation barrier that divided East and West Berlin for 28 years, from 1961 to 1989.

Britain gave up most of its colonies, including India, from 1947. Queen Elizabeth II succeeded her father, King George VI in 1952. In Ireland, the Irish Free State gave up its Commonwealth membership and became a republic on April 1, 1949. Hungary and Italy also became republics. West Germany was established as the Federal Republic of Germany, and East Germany as the Democratic Republic of Germany. In 1991, Germany was reunited as one country. One of the most important events of the 20th century was the breaking up of the Soviet Union in 1991 and the formation of the Russian Federation with 15 independent republics.

The Balkans
In November 1945, the former kingdom of Yugoslavia became the Communist-ruled Federal People's Republic of Yugoslavia. The country consisted of Croatia, Macedonia, Montenegro, Bosnia-Herzegovina, Serbia, and Slovenia. However, in 1991, these countries began fighting each other and by the end of the century, the Federal People's Republic of Yugoslavia was completely destroyed by the bitter racial battles of its people.

Asia
The second half of the 20th century was a period of war, death, and destruction in many parts of Asia. When India, with its Hindu majority, gained independence, Muslim Pakistan was carved out of the northwestern part of the country, as well as a small part in the east. In 1971, East Pakistan broke away and established itself as Bangladesh. In China the civil war that had started in 1929, ended 1949 and the People's Republic of China was established by the Communist Party under Mao-Tse Tung. In 1952, the United States withdrew its forces from Japan. Japan gained complete independence, formed a new constitution and set itself on a path of industrialization and development.

The Middle East
The state of Israel—the world's only Jewish state—was formed in 1948. From the time of its formation, Israel has been engaged in conflicts with the surrounding Arab nations Egypt, Syria, Lebanon, Iraq, and Jordan, as well as with the Palestinian Arabs. Two of the most important conflicts were the Arab-Israeli war of 1948 and the Six-Day War of 1967. In 1958, the Iranian monarchy was overthrown and military rule was established. Between 1980 and 1988, Iraq was at war with Iran. Iraq invaded Kuwait between 1990 and 1991.

rica

1948, the South African government, run descendants of European settlers, established rtheid, a system that separated the untry's peoples and gave privileges to those European origin. After years of struggle, the ican National Congress established a native ican government in 1994, with Nelson ndela as their first president. In Egypt, the narchy was overthrown and a republic was ablished in 1953. In 1956, President Gamal del Nasser nationalized the Suez Canal. This to war with the United Kingdom, France, d Israel, who also used the Suez route.

nericas

e United States of America rose to position of a superpower and became a midable contender in the race to develop werful nuclear weapons. The Civil Rights vement between 1955 and 1968 was a ficult period in the history of the United tes. African Americans protested peacefully inst the racial discrimination and inequality y suffered, which led to great changes in nerican society. Meanwhile, most South nerican countries underwent a period of litical chaos because of a succession of effective military dictatorships. Several untries in this continent suffered long riods of civil war. Cuba became a Communist te in 1959 under the leadership of Fidel stro. It is still the only Communist country the Western Hemisphere.

Mission unforgettable

Vietnam War was fought from 1965 to 1973 between Democratic Republic of Vietnam, which ruled North tnam, and the Viet Cong rebels of South Vietnam. th Vietnam was supported by the United States.

Try these too:

The American Revolution and Civil War (p 16–17), The Second World War (p 22–23)

◄ **Fight against apartheid**
Nelson Mandela spent a large part of his life in prison. His release in 1990 marked the end of apartheid in South Africa.

▼ **A rightful struggle**
African Americans voiced their protests in different ways. They took to the streets demanding equal rights and also organized bus boycotts and sit-ins at restaurants, to abolish racial segregation.

Ethnic wars

The world witnessed an increase in ethnic clashes during the 20th century. An ethnic clash is fighting between two groups of people from the same area, who are racially different, speak different languages, or follow different religions. These battles have often resulted in genocide, or mass killings of people belonging to a particular group. The Hindu-Muslim conflict in India and the Arab-Israeli clash in Palestine are examples of ethnic wars.

The New Millennium

The 21st century has seen a period of relative peace in many parts of the world, but continued violence and bloodshed in others. The world has also had to face new threats and dangers like terrorism and increased global warming.

▶ **Katrina's fury**
The storm surge caused by Hurricane Katrina in August 2005 devastated the city of New Orleans.

In the United States, the new millennium began with the election of George W. Bush as president. The United States faced its worst disaster in recent history on September 11, 2001, when terrorists attacked the twin towers of the World Trade Center in New York and the Pentagon building in Washington. More than 2,700 people were killed in these attacks. In Mexico, Vicente Fox was elected president after the first ever free and fair polls to be held in Mexico. He is also the first opposition leader to be elected, ending the 71-year rule of the Institutional Revolutionary Party.

Europe

In March 2000, the Russian Federation elected Vladimir Putin as their second president. He was also re-elected to the post in 2003. Tony Blair was elected to his second and third terms as the British prime minister in 2001 and 2005. He is the Labor Party's longest-serving leader.

The Union

Europe first came together under the European Coal and Steel Community (ECSC) in 1951. The idea was to promote trade relations between the members and maintain peace in the region. This soon gave way to the European Economic Community in 1958.

▲ **A tribute in light**
Two columns of light are displayed every year at the World Trade Center site to mark the anniversary of the attack.

▲ **The euro**
In 2002, the euro became the common currency of 12 member countries in the European Union.

The EEC expanded over the years and later became the European Union. By 2004 the European Union's membership had increased to 25 countries.

Trouble continues

In the former Yugoslav Republics of Bosnia-Herzegovina and Serbia-Montenegro the violence has continued and these loosely joined federations may be further split in th near future. The former president of Serbia Montenegro, Slobodan Milosevic, was tried by the United Nations for his role in war crimes and mass murders in Kosovo, Serbia

Try these too:

Moving Ahead (p 12–13),
The Computer
Revolution (p 24–25),
The Modern World
(p 26–27)

◄ **Ineffective defense**
The main battle tanks used
by the coalition forces in
the Iraqi invasion were
much more advanced and
reliable than the Iraqi
T-72 tanks. Iraq's artillery
and air defense also
proved to be ineffective
in the face of the advanced
weaponry and attack
aircraft of the coalition.

their mission by Spain, Italy, Portugal, the
Czech Republic, Poland, and Denmark. The
war and subsequent US-led occupation of Iraq
began in March 2003. In December of the
same year the Iraqi dictator Saddam Hussein
was arrested. He was executed in December
2007 after a lengthy trial.

The Middle East

The war between Israel and the
Palestinians continued from the
previous century in spite of
the peacekeeping efforts
of leaders on both sides.
However, in August
2005, in an attempt
to improve relations with the
Palestinians, the Israelis withdrew
from the occupied territory of
the Gaza Strip. In 2003, the
United States and the United
Kingdom jointly declared war
against Iraq, saying Iraq had
failed to prove that it had
destroyed all its biological and
chemical weapons and was not
secretly developing nuclear
weapons. They
were supported in

The Indian subcontinent

In 2004, Pervez Musharraf declared himself
the president of Pakistan. Musharraf, formerly
the Pakistani army chief, had taken control of
the government in a coup at the end of the
20th century. He continues to hold peace
talks with Prime Minister Manmohan Singh,
who heads India's new government, elected to
power in 2004. In 2001, the United States,
supported by the United Kingdom, launched
an attack on Afghanistan to destroy the bases
of the international terrorist group Al-Qaeda,
which was responsible for the September 11
attacks on the World Trade Center and the
Pentagon. The war in Afghanistan led to the
fall of the Islamic Taliban government and the
declaration of the Republic of Afghanistan,
with Hamid Karzai as its first leader.

▼ **For the fear of flu**
In 2005–2006, the world
was gripped by the fear of
bird flu. The H5N1 strain
of the virus is also fatal to
humans. This has led to a
fall in the consumption of
poultry, with thousands
of infected birds being
killed to stop the spread
of infection.

▼ **Killer tsunami**
The killer waves that were
triggered by the earthquake
of December 2004 were up
to 100 feet (30 meters) high
and caused destruction in
12 countries.

Worst disaster of the 21st century

On December 26, 2004, an earthquake
measuring 9.0 on the Richter scale shook
the bed of the Indian Ocean, triggering
a tsunami. Indonesia was the worst
affected, but Thailand, Malaysia, Sri
Lanka, Bangladesh, India, the Maldives,
and even the East African countries of
Kenya, Somalia, and Tanzania felt the
effects of this powerful quake. Over
280,000 people died in this disaster,
more than half of them in Indonesia.

Index